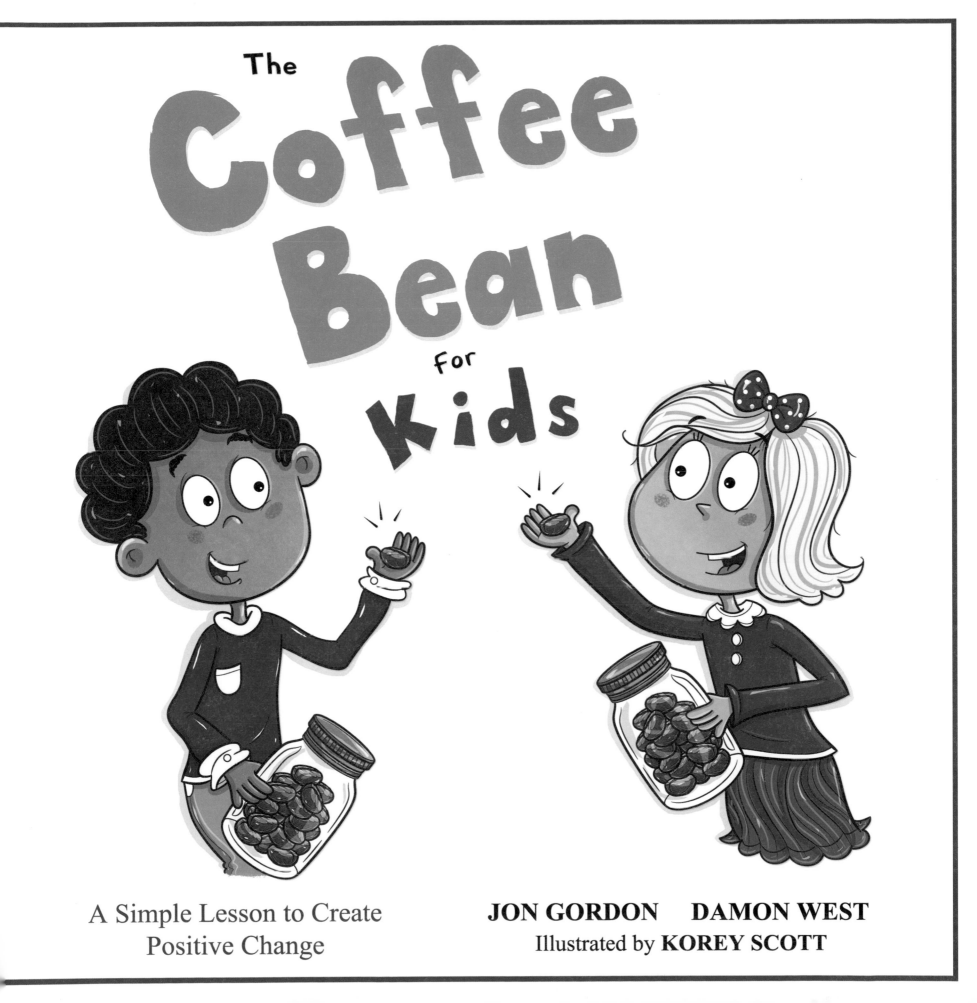

The Coffee Bean for Kids

Kids

A Simple Lesson to Create
Positive Change

JON GORDON   **DAMON WEST**
Illustrated by **KOREY SCOTT**

Published by John Wiley & Sons, Inc., Hoboken, New Jersey.
Published simultaneously in Canada.

For general information on our other products and services or for technical support, please contact our Customer Care Department within the United States at (800) 762-2974, outside the United States at (317) 572-3993 or fax (317) 572-4002.

Wiley publishes in a variety of print and electronic formats and by print-on-demand. Some material included with standard print versions of this book may not be included in e-books or in print-on-demand. If this book refers to media such as a CD or DVD that is not included in the version you purchased, you may download this material at http://booksupport.wiley.com. For more information about Wiley products, visit www.wiley.com.

Library of Congress Cataloging-in-Publication Data:

Names: Gordon, Jon, 1971- author. | West, Damon, author.
Title: The coffee bean for kids / Jon Gordon and Damon West.
Description: Hoboken, New Jersey : Wiley, 2021.
Identifiers: LCCN 2020029669 (print) | LCCN 2020029670 (ebook) | ISBN
    9781119762713 (cloth) | ISBN 9781119762737 (adobe pdf) | ISBN
    9781119762751 (epub)
Subjects: LCSH: Attitude (Psychology)—Juvenile literature. | Positive
    psychology—Juvenile literature. | Self-esteem—Juvenile literature.
Classification: LCC BF327 .G67 2021 (print) | LCC BF327 (ebook) | DDC
    650.1—dc23
LC record available at https://lccn.loc.gov/2020029669
LC ebook record available at https://lccn.loc.gov/2020029670

Cover illustrations: Korey Scott

Printed in the United States of America

10 9 8 7 6 5 4 3 2 1

Gavin used to love going to school, but not this year. He and his family moved to a new city and he had trouble making friends at his new school. Some of the kids also made fun of him because they said he talked funny.

As Gavin walked into his classroom, he saw his teacher, Mrs. Spring, and her smile made him smile. He liked Mrs. Spring's class and wished everyone at school was as nice as her.

When the school day was over, Mrs. Spring asked Gavin to stay after class. Gavin thought he was in trouble. His palms became cold and sweaty, and he could hear his own heart beating.

Mrs. Spring said, "Gavin, I can see that you are not happy. In fact, you look sad. You hardly ever smile, and when you do it's usually only when you say hello to me before class starts. What's wrong, Gavin?"

A few tears came trickling down his face as he told Mrs. Spring about how hard it was to adjust to this new school and make friends.

To make matters worse, his parents were fighting a lot.

Mrs. Spring gave him a big smile and said, "I'm going to share with you one of the best lessons you will ever learn. It's also going to help you make new friends and become a leader for the rest of your life."

Mrs. Spring went to the whiteboard and drew a picture of a pot of boiling water. Then she drew a carrot inside the pot. She asked, "What happens if you put a carrot into a pot of boiling water?"

"You get carrot soup," Gavin said.

Mrs. Spring smiled. "You're on the right track, Gavin, because a carrot turns soft and mushy in a pot of boiling water after a few minutes."

Mrs. Spring then drew another pot of boiling water on the whiteboard. This time, she drew a picture of an egg inside the pot. She asked, "What happens if you put an egg inside a pot of boiling water?"

"That's easy," Gavin said, proudly. "My mom and I did this at Easter. You put the eggs in the pot of boiling water to make the eggs hard, like a hard-boiled egg."

"That is absolutely correct," Mrs. Spring said. "The soft inside of the egg turns hard after a few minutes in a pot of boiling water."

Gavin looked confused. He asked Mrs. Spring how a picture of boiling carrots and eggs could be one of the best lessons he'd ever learned.

"You'll see, Gavin. I have one more example for you." Next to the pots with the carrot and the egg, she drew a third pot of boiling water. This time, she drew a coffee bean inside the pot, and asked Gavin if he knew what happened when you put a coffee bean in boiling water.

"I have no idea," Gavin admitted.

Mrs. Spring explained, "The coffee bean—the smallest of these three things—*changes* the water into coffee. You see, the power to change is inside the coffee bean."

Gavin looked confused. "I don't understand what carrots, eggs, and coffee beans have to do with me fitting in or finding friends," he said.

"Life is often like a pot of very hot water," said Mrs. Spring. "It can be a harsh, stressful, and difficult place. You will find yourself in places and situations that test who you truly are, and can change, weaken, or harden you if you let them."

"Like all the stuff I'm going through now?" Gavin asked.

"Exactly like that, Gavin. You are feeling the pressures of fitting into a new school, the difficulties of finding new friends, and your parents are fighting. You are experiencing fears over things you cannot control, and it feels like you are in one big pot of boiling water. But you do have a choice."

Mrs. Spring

BEST Teacher

"You can be like the carrot that is weakened and softened by its surroundings."

"You can be like the egg that is hardened by the mean people of this world."

"Or you can be like the coffee bean that transforms and changes its environment. When I look at you, I don't see a carrot and I don't see an egg. I see a coffee bean who will overcome challenges and change the world."

That made Gavin smile. "Do you really think I can be a coffee bean?" Gavin asked.

Mrs. Spring smiled. "I know you can be a coffee bean, Gavin. In fact, I want you to remember this lesson for the rest of your life. Wherever you go and whatever you do, remember you are a coffee bean and you have the power to transform any environment you are in."

"No matter how hard things get, or how hopeless things appear, do not ever give up. Realize that we don't create our world from the outside in; we create and transform it from the inside out."

"If you think you are a carrot, you will believe the forces outside of you are stronger than who you are on the inside, and you will become weaker."

"If you think you are the egg, you will believe the mean people in this world have the power to harden your heart and cause you to become negative and angry like they are."

"If you know you are a coffee bean, you will not allow the outside world to affect you. You will know that the power inside you is greater than the forces outside you, and with this insight, you will positively transform your world from the inside out."

14

"The power is on the inside. Be a coffee bean!"

Mrs. Spring then opened a jar on her desk and pulled out a coffee bean. "Keep this in your pocket as a reminder of who you are and the power you have. The best is yet to come for you, Gavin."

BEST
Teacher

Gavin took the coffee bean, told her thank you, and ran excitedly towards the door.

"Wait, Gavin!" Mrs. Spring stopped him. "There's one more thing you need to know. Coffee beans are always smiling, even on the days they do not feel like it. Do you know why?"

"So they can be happy," Gavin said.

Mrs. Spring

BEST
Teacher

"That's right," she said. "It's also for other people to be happy. When people see you smiling, they will smile back. Then other people will see the smiles and they'll start smiling, too. Positive energy and smiling are contagious. Just like when I greet all the kids coming in my door every morning. I'm being a coffee bean so you will all be positive little coffee beans, too. Coffee beans attract other coffee beans! So go now, Gavin. Go be a coffee bean," she said, as Gavin ran out the door.

When Gavin's mother picked him up from school, she noticed how happy and excited he was. She asked him what was different, so he told her all about the coffee bean. "From now on, Mom, I am going to be a coffee bean."

The next day at school, Gavin was all smiles. He noticed that it was working. Other kids were smiling back at him.

When he got to Mrs. Spring's class, he high-fived her with a huge grin on his face. Mrs. Spring knew he was feeling the awesome power of being a coffee bean.

At the end of the week, the snow cone truck came to school. Many of the kids rushed out to buy one. Gavin was standing in line for his snow cone and noticed a kid with special needs standing alone. He had an idea.

He went over to Mrs. Spring and asked if he could use his snow cone money to buy the other kid a snow cone. Mrs. Spring smiled and told him that it would absolutely be okay. "That is definitely a coffee bean thing to do," she told him.

Gavin was a little nervous about meeting a new kid, but he went over to the boy to introduce himself. Before he could say a word, the boy smiled and stuck his hand out. "Hi! My name is Michael," he said. "What's your name?"

This was easier than Gavin thought. Michael was really friendly. Gavin shook Michael's hand. "I'm Gavin," he replied. "Do you want a snow cone?"

Michael kept smiling and nodded his head up and down. "I love snow cones," he said.

Gavin and Michael walked over to the snow cone truck to buy Michael a snow cone. Gavin didn't get to eat a snow cone because he only had enough money for one, but the best treat of all was watching how happy Michael was eating his snow cone.

CONE

"Wow," Gavin thought to himself. "Being a coffee bean feels good."

A few days later, Gavin was at lunch, sitting quietly by himself like he always did. But even though no one else sat with him, he was not sad. In fact, he was smiling, just like Mrs. Spring told him to do. As he was opening his lunch kit, he noticed a girl standing next to him.

"Hi, I'm Clara. Do you want to sit with my friends and me?" she asked.

Gavin couldn't believe it. Clara was one of the smartest and prettiest girls in fourth grade. They were in Mrs. Spring's class together, but they had never talked to each other. Now, she was asking him to sit with her friends. "Um, sure," he said.

Clara walked with Gavin to the table where she ate with her friends. She introduced Gavin to each one of them. "Gavin, these are my friends, Peter, Maya, and Priya. Everybody, this is Gavin."

Everyone smiled and said hello. As soon as Gavin sat down, all the kids took turns talking to him. He barely had a chance to eat his lunch because there was so much conversation. Gavin could not believe his luck. Until today, he had no friends. Now, he had a table full of new friends.

When the table got quiet, he asked Clara, "Why is everybody being so nice to me?"

All the kids at the table looked at Clara. She smiled and said, "We noticed you've been smiling a lot, and looking for ways to help others. Like the other day, when you bought Michael a snow cone. That was very kind. My mother tells me all the time that being kind is the best thing you can be and that it's a choice. We are always looking for other kind kids to be our friends."

Gavin knew he had made his new friends because of his choice to be a coffee bean. "I'm a coffee bean," he said. "It sounds like you are all coffee beans, too."

The kids looked confused, so Clara asked Gavin what it meant to be a coffee bean.

Gavin told everyone at the table about the lesson Mrs. Spring taught him, about the carrot, the egg, and the coffee bean, and about how being a coffee bean would attract other coffee beans and create positivity.

That gave Clara an idea. "Gavin, this is something we should share with all the kids in school. In fact, we could start a coffee bean club, and go find other coffee beans. We could turn this whole school into one big pot of coffee!"

After school, Clara and Gavin talked to Mrs. Spring about the Coffee Bean Club. Mrs. Spring thought it was a great idea and they agreed the club would meet before school started.

Clara, Gavin, and their friends began telling everyone about the first Coffee Bean Club meeting. They made flyers and went around telling kids in every grade about the carrot, the egg, and the coffee bean.

At lunch the day before the first meeting, they even made a coffee bean song.

When the morning for the first meeting finally arrived, Clara and her mom, Mrs. Kendell, arrived at Mrs. Spring's classroom extra early with some healthy snacks they had made the night before. When the kids started arriving, Mrs. Spring was all smiles, as usual.

Everyone was surprised by how many kids showed up for the first meeting of the Coffee Bean Club. Gavin was so excited to see Michael show up, too.

"Hey, Gavin. My mom said I could be a coffee bean, too," Michael said, proudly.

Mrs. Spring started the meeting by telling everyone, "The main goals of our club are to be kind to everyone and always to be positive."

Next, Mrs. Spring told students that they needed to come up with rules for the Coffee Bean Club.

Clara raised her hand. "I think the first rule should be 'Help others,'" she said. "This means that you look for carrots and eggs and try to help them become coffee beans, too."

The kids clapped in approval, so Mrs. Spring wrote on the board:

Rule #1. Help others.

Gavin raised his hand next. "Include everybody," he said. "This means that anyone who wants to be in the club can join. It also means that when someone wants to join in and play a game or sit at your lunch table, then they can do that, too. More coffee beans make our pot of coffee stronger."

Coffee Bean
Club
Rule #1 - Help Others
Rule #2 - Include Everybody

The COFFEE BEAN Club

Again, the kids clapped in approval. They added a second rule to the board:

Rule #2. Include everybody.

Maya was called on next. "The third rule should be to smile, because smiles are like boomerangs," she said. "When you smile, it always comes back to you. You smile at someone and they smile back."

Rule #1 - Help Others
Rule #2 - Include Everybody
Rule #3 - Smile

"Smiles make me happy," said Michael, as Mrs. Spring wrote on the board: *Rule #3. Smile.*

After the three rules of the Coffee Bean Club were on the board, Clara raised her hand.

"Mrs. Spring, we made a song for the club. Can we sing it?" she asked.

Rule #1 - Help Others
Rule #2 - Include Everybody
Rule #3 - Smile

"Of course you can," Mrs. Spring said. "How exciting."

Clara, Gavin, Peter, Maya, Priya, and Michael all went to the front of the room and began to sing.

The room erupted with cheers and clapping. Then the kids started chanting,

The Coffee Bean Club made it their mission to find coffee beans all over their school. They wrote positive notes to students who seemed to be having a tough time and they engaged in random acts of kindness. Over the course of the rest of the school year, it was clear to all that the Coffee Bean Club positively changed the school. In fact, the club became so big that they had to hold their monthly meetings in the gymnasium.

Everyone wanted to be in the Coffee Bean Club.

Everyone wanted to be a coffee bean.

It was no longer cool to be negative or mean. Instead, it became cool to be a coffee bean and help others.

THE END

BRING *THE COFFEE BEAN* TO YOUR SCHOOL

For tools and resources to bring The Coffee Bean to your school, visit:

   CoffeeBeanKidsBook.com

Resources include:

- Videos
- Teacher guide
- Student action plan
- Coffee Bean Club Kit (materials to create a Coffee Bean Club in your school)
- Assemblies and workshops

OTHER BOOKS BY THE AUTHORS

The Coffee Bean

From bestselling author Jon Gordon and rising star Damon West comes *The Coffee Bean*: an illustrated fable that teaches readers how to transform their environment, overcome challenges, and create positive change.

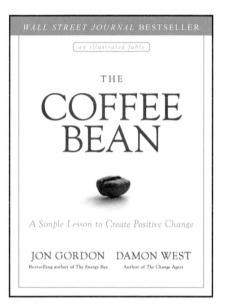

Life is often difficult. It can be harsh, stressful, and feel like a pot of boiling hot water. The environments we find ourselves in can change, weaken, or harden us, and test who we truly are. We can be like the carrot that weakens in the pot or like the egg that hardens. Or, we can be like the coffee bean and discover the power inside us to transform our environment.

The Coffee Bean is an inspiring tale that follows Abe, a young man filled with stress and fear as he faces challenges and pressure at school and home. One day after class, his teacher shares with him the life-changing lesson of the coffee bean, and this powerful message changes the way he thinks, acts, and sees the world. Abe discovers that instead of letting his environment change him for the worse, he can transform any environment he is in for the better. Equipped with this transformational truth, Abe embarks on an inspirational journey to live his life like the coffee bean. Wherever his life takes him, from school, to the military, to the business world, Abe demonstrates how this simple lesson can unleash the unstoppable power within you.

A delightful, quick read, *The Coffee Bean* is purposely written and designed for readers of all ages so that everyone can benefit from this transformational lesson. This is a book and message that, when read and shared, has the power to change your life and the world around you. You just have to decide: are you a carrot, egg, or coffee bean?

www.CoffeeBeanBook.com

OTHER CHILDREN'S BOOKS BY JON GORDON

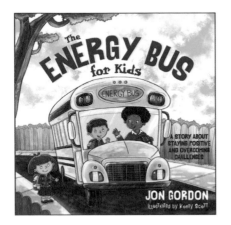

The Energy Bus for Kids

The illustrated children's adaptation of the bestselling book *The Energy Bus* tells the story of George, who, with the help of his school bus driver, Joy, learns that if he believes in himself, he'll find the strength to overcome any challenge. His journey teaches kids how to overcome negativity, bullies, and everyday challenges to be their best.

www.EnergyBusKids.com

Thank You and Good Night

Thank You and Good Night is a beautifully illustrated book that shares the heart of gratitude. Jon Gordon takes a little boy and girl on a fun-filled journey from one perfect moonlit night to the next. During their adventurous days and nights, the children explore the people, places, and things they are thankful for.

OTHER CHILDREN'S BOOKS BY JON GORDON

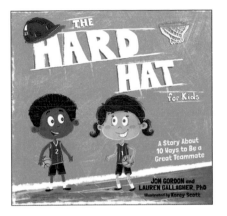

The Hard Hat for Kids

The Hard Hat for Kids is an illustrated guide to teamwork. Adapted from the bestseller *The Hard Hat*, this uplifting story presents practical insights and life-changing lessons that are immediately applicable to everyday situations, giving kids—and adults—a new outlook on cooperation, friendship, and the selfless nature of true teamwork.

www.HardHatforKids.com

One Word for Kids

If you could choose only one word to help you have your best year ever, what would it be? *Love? Fun? Believe? Brave?* It's probably different for everyone. How you find your word is just as important as the word itself. And once you know your word, what do you do with it? In *One Word for Kids*, bestselling author Jon Gordon—along with coauthors Dan Britton and Jimmy Page—asks these questions to children and adults of all ages, teaching an important life lesson in the process.

www.getoneword.com/kids

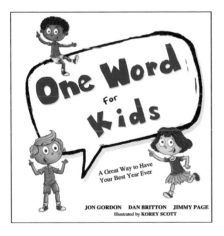